This Garden

Dan Lewis

ISBN 978-1-105-20071-7

Publshed by Lulu.com

Cover photo: Marina Castillo Photography
Interior drawing: Marye Goodrich McKenney
Cover design and author photo by the author

for Ann
all ways

Contents

III

IV

Acknowledgements

The author wishes to thank the following publications in which these poems first appeared:

Beloit Poetry Journal: Calder

Blue Unicorn: Chimera

Café Review: In-Orbit Repairs

Cutbank: Chelydra serpentina

Diner: Manifesto; For Ann; Wild Ride; Libby Museum; The Net is Everywhere Conjoined; Valentine; Souvenir; Experiments in Abstraction

Eclectica: Watching the Astronauts—ISS March, 2001

The Hopkinton Crier: Great Blue

Magnapoets: Boundary Street; Closing the Camp

New Verse News: Jihad

November 3rd Club: Rant for a Rusty Kazoo

The New Worcester Spy: Four Night Songs; Etude at 3 a.m.; Entr'acte; Balloon:

Paper Street Press: The Sound of Glass

Sahara: Aha #2858; Paying Attention; Charlie's Birds; Logos; Camera Obscura

Segue: We Who Once Lived in This House of Stars; Spring in the Emerald City

Southern New Hampshire University Journal: The Face That Will Not Come Off; Grapes

Sun's Skeleton: Old Penny; There Goes the Neighborhood

Worcester Magazine: Flashlights

The Worcester Review: Recoil; Prime Meridian

Special thanks to Susan Roney O'Brien, John Hodgen, and Gene McCarthy. Their assistance with the manuscript and their continuing friendship are gifts beyond reckoning.

Manifesto

This is exactly what I mean. In the middle
of the half-acre dump, piled with broken bricks, old tires,
and the street sweeper's waste, two bright sunflowers
stand beatified in the slant light of morning.
We must over and over again bear witness
to the wonder of this world. After the bone-rich
ash is shoveled from the ovens, after the scarred witnesses
have told their terrible tales, after the weapons have been gathered
and burned, someone must still have voice to sing. This
is the only ground we have to stand on, this
scorched and defiled garden. It is here we must raise
the cry until our throats tear with the fierce hymn of praise.

I

Recoil

When it comes it will be, I think,
like the kick
of my father's twelve gauge shotgun
when I was nine. Anticipated glory, it exploded
inside my body, surprising sinew, unbuckling
my joints. I would have fallen backward
but my father's hewn hands, firm
on my shoulders held me fast to the world.

Now fifty yards into the woods and coughing again,
he leans unsteadily against a tree and waits
for the spasm to pass.
Extra innings
is what the doctor says we have of him now.
Extra innings, the measured part of the game
concluded, the rulebook suspended,
the crowd antsy in their seats.

Doubtless he should not be walking in the woods at all,
though I likely should not have panicked five minutes ago
finding him suddenly gone from the porch.
He will sit now on a boulder,
to tease a tendril of breath out of the thin air
shaking his head at me, sheepish
as if this weakness were his own doing.
But he is tired; the pretense will not hold
he will walk back to the house slowly
leaning on my arm.

The first time I fired the shotgun
it was exactly as I thought it would be, exactly,
except that nothing could have prepared me
for that fierce blow, delivered from nowhere
that I could see. Obdurate, intractable, more genuine
than any seen thing. It was not the force,
but the sudden clear knowledge
that knocked the wind out of me.

Charlie's Birds

The thing is, the bird does not PUSH
itself through the air, using its wings
like oars; the wings PULL
the bird, biting the air
like propellers.

Lift, thrust—drag, gravity
wing—bird.

The old cliché then is correct; the bird IS on the wing.

What then is flight:
        applications of the laws of physics?
        aerodynamic engineering?
        a blind urgency for weightlessness?

And what are the curvatures of air this morning
that make progress upward and into the wind a downhill glide?

These motions are part of a matrix.
My watching of a single tree swallow,
recognizable because it is missing a primary
from its left wing (and this, amazingly,
does not visibly impede its flight!)
yields little more clue
than a plastic wind-up bird
launched from a child's hand.

These at the very least the model must include:
bird, bird, bird, and bird;
a landscape—some track of air
that is memory of landscape—a complex
three dimensional map;
currents, eddies, gusts (one of which,
hit wrong, hit with the minutest error
of wing or tail,
would erase flight and tumble a confusion of feathers to the ground);
contours of earth and air; gravity;
pressure; volume; weight
(an assembly of hollow struts—
bird bone—feather shaft—air).

Internal chemistry: food; water; oxygen.
Process: territory, pairing, nest building, copulation.
Internal architecture: neuron, synapse:
electricity exploding (with the help
of millennia of cellular experimentation)
into flight.

How many swallows missed the gnat
and starved, or turned wrong angle to the wind
to be dashed to earth before this one learned to fly?

I cannot believe that an infinite number of monkeys with an infinite
number of tinkertoy sets could ever build a tree swallow.

Cannot believe, but know, see,
as I see the bird glide INTO the wind.

The Net is Everywhere Conjoined

There is no wind
only this wash of rain
filling the courtyard—
its brickwet smell, its liquid
music. And the ivy on the walls,
big, waxy leaves with long
petioles; how they move
passing rainwater from leaf to leaf.

But what *is* this that lies
outside?—is there anything
outside? of this bone walled
cranial closet we call
self? Surely it seems so; everything
in here seems to point
outward, and the body, muttering
to itself, maintains a steady
monologue of contact. But what
sort of thing *is*
it? Not filtered, I mean, by the
senses? not perceived by any
of the means we have to perceive
it; the thing in itself—inscrutable
as god. Where does it live?

Look then at the motion of this wall.
Where it starts, up under the dripping

eaves—too high to see clearly—
driven only by gravity—
the need of the rain to
fall, of water to find
its own level. Nearer the bottom,
where I am standing, it is possible to see
what happens: each leaf a vessel with three
spouts, each capable of holding just
so much (determined by a complex
congruence of area, center
of gravity, stiffness of stem, even
the surface tension of the rainwater itself) before a drop
poured from a tilting spout above tips
the delicate balance and the leaf
dips, or twists, or bends downward
to spill the load from one of its
three lobes (which lobe becomes
the path of release also determined
by a complex interaction involving
the shape of the blade, the position
that the water strikes it, the motion
it retains from the previous event),
so that the whole wall is a dance in which
patterns form, merge, and fade to
reform, shifting rhythms, undulations,
punctuated by occasional staccato
splashes (where, for instance, one leaf
is hit by large drops from two
directions at once).

Is there structure here? information?
a level of meaning that overlays

the simple material facts of
brick wall, ivy, and falling rain?
Is this how the courtyard
thinks? What is it thinking
now? Is this thinking separate
from my thinking? Has my watching
and watching merged our minds
in the short space of my watching?
So that I can claim it? Like these
mutable linkings and relinkings
I claim because their substrate is inside my
skull?

How many such structures are there? Where
is their interface? In what
sort of consciousness might they
collect? These words, spun
from my looking, themselves a sort of
structure, have some capacity
to connect, to propagate what is,
if nothing else, the result of my
looking, the result of at least the
existence of pattern—this rain, this
wall, what happens
here.

Pike's Peak, May, 1997

Consider a twenty-four inch cogged wheel,
case-hardened, fifteen deep teeth, slightly
rounded. The whole five inches thick but
formed in two parts as if
split against the axis—one half
rotated twelve degrees—so that,
engaging the split rack
the wheel maintains its grip, one cog
always fully inserted.

The vibration is not surprising.

High meadow and summit attainable
in nearly direct line. (From my parents' deck,
seen through binoculars, the cograil path
is nearly invisible.)

So we ascend,
rattling, hauled upward,
held fast to a steel chord.

Always I assumed that one day
I would shoulder a pack,
and walk up here alone, was certain, in fact
that I would ultimately be absorbed
into these mountains, traveling light,
living off the land.

I saw myself in a photograph
just above treeline, boots trail-scuffed,
backpack and shoulder, worn
to each other's shape, permanent sunsquint
under a weatherbeaten hat.

I somehow didn't understand
that you must surrender at least
the world
to climb alone
to this altitude
where everything
falls away.

Yesterday we brought mother home
with sixty feet of plastic tube,
the definition of her freedom,
coiled in a plastic bag.
Carefully we paced distances,
bed to bathroom
bathroom to closet, closet to kitchen, the stove,
the sink, her easy chair,
the television, and at the full extent of hose,
the window's wide view of mountains.
(She would insist, after all, that the view
is the reason for all of it, that at sea level
she would find sufficient breath.)
We made for her a sort of map,

left side of the couch, right
of kitchen counter, always return
the same way you came, watch
always for kinks.

From Manitou Springs
upward into wood and rock and air and light
we are hauled, knee to knee
with other tourists, staring
into the quick glimpsed spaces of imagined wilderness
until our eyes burn.

The woods fall away now.
We are inside a cloud
that is lined with gravel
and thin spikes of grass.
What happens to space
at this altitude? Distance
is recalculated—some warp of time or gravity.
Over the brim of this meadow
the lower world
is light years distant.

I no longer believe
I could live on rainwater and stones,
cannot pretend even
that any foreseeable future
contains this rarefied wealth of landscape.

At summit house
outside the gift shop
I drop a quarter in a binocular turret
and try to glimpse backward
down the mountain, try to find
the speck that would be
my parents' house, that window
where I am certain
my mother is standing now
at the full extent of her tether
looking up.

7 June

Outside.
Through the window
of the restaurant where I
eat alone. Last light of the
day and the street—all of this
(as if I could tell you; could
in fact snag it in this airy net
of words) vivid. Because something
will happen. Here. In this
life. Because something has
happened before—something but
not exactly what you expected—what
did you expect? Last light. Yes and
summer—short sleeves—how your
feet feel in the sandals again. See for example
the three women on the steps
of Mount Olive Pentecostal Church, their
white dresses so white, and a boy, maybe
two or three, waving his hands, doing jerky dance
steps and the women their large
bodies shaking with pleasure—in this
summer—no, almost summer—
night. Or here on the side street now three
boys pile out of a car with grocery
bags, yellow plastic bulging, and
carry them to the door of a
three-decker—yes, like that—something

will happen. Nineteen sixty eight,
Hartford, Connecticut, you are
twenty-one and certain your life
is about to begin. Summer evening, or almost
summer. Something will happen—the
boy has stopped his dance now, the
women move toward the door of the
church. Maybe it has already happened,
maybe that is why you know it
already, maybe it is only
your life.

Camera Obscura

What can we do here? just after
sunset? Contained within the limits
of ourselves. No way out
of the cave, the screen clouded
by impatient breaths, the eager
press of so many hands.
         A swan now,
its white shocking against
the dark surface
of the lake, its wings a shower
of terrible blessings. Must it
matter then? that this light
is the very last?

Watching the Astronauts
International Space Station, March, 2001

Is this what the body dreams for itself—
to float like Chagall's lover, propelled
by whim or intention to any curvature
of space? Here on the earth where
weight defines us and things stay
where they are put—rock solid,
sure footed, feet-on-the-ground, we watch rapt,
the erratic path of a wind-drift
plastic bag above a gusty city street.
Or falling asleep, we learn again
to fly. Between the prebirth amniotic lilt
and the final matterless floating away, we learn
to praise and curse the time-bound
present, with its awful weight of being.
Dreaming always of height and distance
we build pyramids, obelisks, steeples; loft
kites, balloons, airplanes, and now, built
on the broken bones of centuries, this
improbable assembly of space-borne tin cans
in which a chosen few are permitted, for
a time at least, to defy all laws and float free
with their astonished bodies.

Tracery

Start with the arc of the line,
not parabolic, not sinusoidal, only
the trailing curve tracing trajectory
of the cast bait. Just after
sunrise of a grey day—how
the line itself catches
the light, glows pink against
a leaden sky.

                         In the hospital
we watch the wave patterns, also
not parabolic, not sinusoidal, that
trace the impulse of her failing heart.
What is this precise calligraphy
whose meaning we try to
bend to our will? What math must
we learn to reshape these arcs?
In that narrow room we can only
stare and count the spiky
peaks and wait for change.

                         The body learns
the motions slowly, and with deliberate
repetition—how the torso twists,
shifting weight to the right
foot, how the arms lift slightly
as the shoulder cocks the cast,
and then the practiced shift

of weight, bringing the arms around,
with a half-step forward to the left
foot, while hands recall a precise
choreography of motions—is this
actual—is this happening
now? What is now? In this place? What
place? Sunrise, yes, Truro, yes, on that
arm of the world reaching—seawater,
saline solution, platelets, whole
blood—into the sea, where the plug
lands, sixty yards out. And now the hands
know to shift position, to grasp
the crank, to flip the bail, to reel in the
slack, pulling the collapsed arc
down out of the sky. All of this the body
knows, as it knows to bring the rod butt
down against the right leg, to slide
the left hand upward to a firm grip above
the reel, to lift the rod tip just so, to
pull line up out of the water, to jerk
the plug so that it splashes just
so and to repeat this pumping
motion with slightly varying
cadence, as if the bait were really
frightened bait *fish* leaping out of
the water.

What change? In the waiting room
nothing is new; only the television lamely
attempting to imitate the thing we think
is life, only our conversation, hushed
by the dim lights, the late hour, the grim
news. We are as good at this game

as any, and as bad, flirting with truth, seeking
bargaining room, trying to create
a familiar space in this
landscape where there are no
rules.

          When the fish strikes, it is announced
by the splash—a sudden out-of-sequence
spray beside the bait, as if the plug itself
had come to life. Now the body does something
new, as if the heart stopped briefly, a caught
breath, adrenaline tensing all muscles.
Without thought, the left hand slides
down to lift the rod upward; the right hand
steadies the crank, thumb extending
to flip the drag lock; all of this just
in time, before the curve flattens
and the taut line strains
against the sudden surprising weight
that bends the rod (this is a new
curve, not stable, oscillating) as the
fish, diving to gain full purchase of the
water's grasp, tests tensile of the line, making
the reel sing. And this too the mind
remembers, how the precarious
thread holds; how it transmits to rod, and
hand, the thrumming engine of the living
fish.

          It is harder now. There is
commitment; there is
no turning back. Once the bait
is taken, once the hook is

set, the fish is everything, which means
what you hold onto, what
holds you to the world, what
finally this world is about. The line
itself, the reel and the rod to which it
is attached are no longer
your own; even your frail
body is not truly your own now. You cannot
see the fish, although its strength
pulses through the singing
line, which means this is as close
as you may come, touching but not
touching (the hand of Adam, for
example, on the ceiling of the Sistine
chapel, or Moses in the cleft
rock). And where now is she while
the machine does her breathing?
Can she hear your voice; does she
know about any of this? Which means
you can only act out this part now
lifting the tip of the rod when the fish
turns, reeling in the hard-won
slack, returning the line to
its tight coil. Only this is your
prayer.   Which means
when the thin tracing on the
monitor goes flat for the last
time (how many times?) you
are there, which means
nothing—and everything there is.

Libby Museum

All these delicate bones—
and such patience—to have dissolved
away the flesh, to have cleaned and
laid them out, to have fit them
back together with such care,
pinning the spidery ribs of the weasel
to the breastbone, threading vertebrae
on fine wire like beads,
re-inventing gesture in the just-so
placement of the red squirrel legbones.
Look how cleverly the plastron
of the painted turtle has been hinged
open to show its skeleton—see
how the vertebrae are fused
to the shell, how in fact the shell
itself is really backbone, grown out
and around. Look how the pelvis and neck
appear helplessly pinned
to the broad inflexible wall.

What are these elaborate armatures
over which our skin is stretched? How can
these creaky machines bear our weight
into the world? What blind
watchmaker or Rube Goldberg
think-alike might conceive
such ingenious and improbable

assemblies? How is it possible, in fact
that we live here at all. Think
of a mirror—think of the eye, unflinching
staring back at the eye that you believe
resides in your own head—think how
desperately you want to know
what this world is. Think
how structure is created and recreated
in your own cerebrum—think
of the delicate mental surgery
that separates the outline of the tree
from the backdrop of the sky. Neurons
build these shapes, like variations
on the theme of ribcage and limb in
the crawling and the walking and
the standing up. You know already
in fact, what God is thinking;
it is precisely, at least in part,
what you are thinking now.

Chelydra serpentina

Then along the side of the road there's this
turtle, and it's just sitting there, head
half out of its shell, not moving, so you think
maybe it's dead—except that its stillness
is taut with potential.
                              Seemingly oblivious
to the leaves and sticks plastered
to its carapace, it waits for some minute
diurnal click to signal now inside
its ancient brain, to wake the lumbering
gait with which it will retrace
its own journey from the egg, down
the mossy hill to the green, skulking pond.

Great Blue

Old patriarch of the bowed wings wide as death,
the pond belongs to you
now that the geese have flown. Dry seedpods
rattle where you land at water's edge, and ancient memories
sleep in the scarecrow of your bones.

Four Night Songs

I keep listening
to the same
frog on the same
night telling me
to start listening.

Someone
has cut
pieces out of the
sky to make a
tent. And now
it keeps on
raining
all the time.

You can't be three
places at twice
once
you move outside
your own head.

❖

Bullfrogs
on the south side of the cove
exchange complex
mathematical constructs
with bullfrogs on the north
side. The bridge
they are building
blots out the moon.

For Ann—June 4, 1999

I have been thinking lately
about who I am—I mean
not that little man who I often imagine
lives somewhere upstairs, feverishly
working the wheels and levers of my brain,
watching the movie, keeping track
or not, of sight and sound and touch and smell;
not the genie in the bottle of my brain
but my brain itself, the thing
I know is, after all, both bottle and genie.

As near as I can understand it
what I am is not so much
the parts (neurons and chemical
transmitters) as the linkings
made and remade and rearranged—
a mutable network of interconnections
that somehow constitute
who it is who wakes
in this budburst green spring morning
with you beside me.
Connections remade frequently enough
form pathways—receptors stimulated
very many times by the same axons
are more easily stimulated in the future.
So patterns are formed, become linked.
The map grows deeper and more complex.

For more than half my life
I have been weaving you into this net.

What happens when I stand up, cross
a room, open a door, or when I simply breathe
this morning air, is neither more nor less
than the singing of these evolving
and intertwining structures.

The touch of your hand on my shoulder
then, my perception of it, resonates
deeply in this unfathomable complexity.
Which synapses are you and which are me?

Love, the truth is, there is no-one watching the movie.
The genie is out of the bottle; there is no way to tease apart
the strands of these patterns, no conceivable way
that I can ever again be a me without being an us.

Paying Attention

Striking the teaspoon
in the empty cereal bowl, the tapwater
glances off, arcs gracefully,
and lands, of course,
on my clean shirt. How many
times have I done this? In my mind
the water hangs suspended, a silver
ameboid globule. Do I flinch
before it hits me, before it hits
the spoon, maybe even before
I turn on the tap, or put the bowl in the sink?
Surely a structure linking act with outcome
must reside somewhere in my brain.
I imagine the homunculus of that thought
shaking its head, even as I eat, saying,
"oh, now here it comes again, watch,
watch; look what we will do." Maybe
it even tries to warn, "hey, hey, remember:
spoon, bowl, flying water—you,
dolt, dimwit," but whatever voice
that synaptic construct may have, is lost
in the crackling neural firestorm: checking
the clock, calculating the day's weather, indulging
imaginary conversations, listening always
to the verbal static of self.
Maybe the homunculus has learned
the futility of shouting into that weather, maybe

it just sits and waits, or maybe
it's smart enough to call ahead to memory,
requesting the location of a new clean shirt.

No matter—I'll know soon enough,
in the inevitable instant
all noise is stunned silent
by the cold, wet slap
smack in the middle
of Monday.

Logos

Researchers say they have slowed light to a dead stop, stored it and then released it as if it were an ordinary material particle.

—New York Times, *Jan. 18, 2001*

If light
can be
stopped
in its
tracks—not
simply absorbed
or reflected
but stopped stone cold—
trapped in a box
by a clever
magician with
a tuned laser—
what then?
And who
could own
such a box?
Surely
no one
that I know
surely
not you
or anyone
like you
or I

firm planted
on this
planet
and thinking
we know
almost
everything.
Here then
is the
captured Word
frozen
in time
too heavy
to lift.

Wild Ride

In the dream Einstein drives
like a maniac. And we,
desperately trying to cling
to composure, and watching
the tumblepast world swallow us,
think this will be, of course,
a story to tell to grandchildren: how
Albert drove—would we call him
Albert?—the stuff of legend surely,
and no notion how it came to pass, but
already pregnant with possibility:
how, for instance, the father
of the modern notion of gravity
appeared to have so little regard
for gravity itself—and then as if
the ground has opened, we drop
into a tunnel whose walls seem broken
by stained glass windows and Albert
drives us to the very edge
of freefall, blurring the colors
in the headlong rush, barely making
the twists and turns, and clearly
having the last laugh, as
this particular wormhole
spits me out into the pale
wakeful light of morning.

II

Souvenir

This is not really a poem.
The thing is I have been given
a memento. It is, in fact, a pear
from the tree that Stanley Kunitz planted in the backyard
of his mother's house when he was a boy—the same tree celebrated
in the poem, *My Mother's Pears.*
Small and already ripe, stems carefully dipped in wax,
more than 50 of them were graciously presented
to guests at the dedication
of a bronze plaque marking that same house.

My problem is this: what does one do
with a memento that is inherently perishable?
This is not an abstract question;
I mean what am I going to do with the goddamn pear?
I suppose I might have it bronzed, but
I have no knowledge of such a process and no idea
whether it is feasible, and if it is, I sincerely doubt
the resultant paperweight would bear much resemblance
the fruit the poem insists is "Worcester's pride."
I have a sculptor friend with a particular knack
for encasing once ephemeral objects in
ponderous blocks of resin.
But a giant's keychain fob seems equally wrong.
If I leave it where it sits on the desk,
where I have watched three days of mid-September light
wash its mottled skin, it will shrivel and spoil.

It is after all not the fruit of my labor;
the holes I dug were never deep enough.
Whatever meager harvests I have made
have been haphazard, undisciplined, and weak.

There's nothing left then I suppose but to eat the thing
reverently, with bowed head, incanting with each bite,
I am not worthy, I am not worthy.

Aha #2858

Now I see—
it's about mind—it's
about structure, about
neural pathways and connections—
what in fact creates
the world we think we see. Adjust
the angle of the lens; see
the optometrist; blink
rapidly; believe in abstraction—
the world new-made at each breath,
conjured out of the delicate cacophony
raised by very many billion neurons
all talking at once.
                    Line,
color, volume, weight, even
the smell of the paint, all
forming and reforming the mutable
flickering fabric of consciousness.
Look, that splash of pure color
invades the space; think
of the brief neural structure
it precipitates; feel
how your mind is bent,
spun, turned by whatever
slap or dash of brush
invites the headlong rush
of neuron firings that makes
these walls sing.

                    Not that cheap
trick of simply jogging
your memory to re-imagine
what you already know, this stuff
wants something new to happen
in the three-pound universe
between your ears.

Worthington Whittredge—"Kaaterskill Falls"
Hudson River School Exhibition, Worcester Art Museum, 1999

Materials then—truth in the concrete—
a catalog: rock first
in all its forms, and water
and light and air,
fundamentals of geology—do not forget
the long lost sheets of ice,
impossibly thick to scour out
this broad gorge,
and then the carbon ring
self-enchanted into reproductive riot
threw up ferns, mosses, grass,
an extravagance of soft tissue
to split rock, create soil:
earth, air, water, and finally
stem, branch, leaf, flower.

But what the eye sees
is only light, filtered by wavelength
to carry a message of these things.
Lens, retina, axon,
thalamus, cortex, the image projected
on the retinal screen
is disassembled in the brain,
becomes a diffuse constellation of states
which cannot, we think, be localized.
Yet whatever they are,
they have been with us a long time,

these states of being that define landscape,
deeply folded into our brains
since our ancestors climbed
down from the trees.

Materials then—
fibers of flax, washed and combed,
spun into strong thread and woven
tightly to a stiff cloth, then stretched
over a wood frame, and spread
with a glue extracted from the hide of a rabbit.
Oxide of titanium, ground in mortar to a fine powder
to be suspended like white jewel dust
in clear viscous oil.

And here, no more godlike hand imaginable
than the one which placed
the rice grain of solid white pigment
precisely here, defining in a single stroke
sunglint on the lip of the waterfall
the focal point of the world.

Experiments in Abstraction
Modernism and Abstraction Exhibition, Worcester Art Museum, 2001

Apology

Throw words up on these walls
in a good light and do not be dogged
by a need for meaning. I'm going to blow
this riff out of the saxophone I always
dreamed of playing. If paint can be poured
from a can onto the canvas, if red itself is a topic,
if the picture can be torn from its frame
and hung to blow in the wind, then maybe words
can be liberated from the tight
commercial fist of syntax.

Thus: Thistle. Delphinium.
Porcupine. Waiting for the promise of
light. A memory of birdsong. Chrysanthemum.
Reaching all the way to the back
of the mailbox. Acrid smell of brass. October.
All decisions postponed.

Teaspoon. Chandelier. Elephant. Majolica.
Searching for handholds. Astronomy. Bearing
the weight of consciousness. Catechism. If.
Then. Otherwise. The clocks are deliberately set
to spread out the time of their striking. Promissory.
Promiscuous. Thrust. Before breakfast; before
lunch; before dinner before…. Say something.
Extrapolating geometry from vision. No comment.
Earth. Stone. Solitude. Silence.

recapitulation   brass buttons   cuspidor
the eyes of the doll remain closed
when the doll cries   Diaghelev
Nijinsky.   ivory carefully salvaged
from the keys of old pianos.
coin silver   how the voice wavers
from the horn of the old
victrola.   heartwood   hammer
the numerals are missing   no one
in the teller's cage   elasticity
percolator   premonition   call me
Tuesday   dustbin   thimble   all of this
impossibly apothecary.

break rhythm   split stick   whipcrack
angelus   dumbstruck against the broken
clockface   everything falling into place
this is what I mean but cannot
sing   this pounding of the blood
harpsichord   garterbelt   meaning   meaning
meaning matterless wrench ratcheting
upward   key in the lock   hands
of the clock   now beat back all dark
music trailing off to this still
insistent pulse   pachyderm
camelot   cornucopia

This is not about
anything outside itself. This
is not about
anything. This
is not outside.
This is not
about. This
is not
This is
This.

Two Poems for Gertrude Halstead

On the occasion of her ninetieth birthday

Kite Flier

To change the shape of air. To
reinvent the center. To become
the point of contact and the point
of departure. To learn to ride
the weather. To read the infinite
in the minutest vibrations
of a taut string.

Water Ouzel

What breaks the surface,
remains, obdurate
as truth;
fierce acrobat, it flashes liquid
through the rushing
crystal world, attains
the air, and
leaves behind,
only
light.

Philippe Petit

That
conundrum which he
proposes is not
new, is not grand, is not
especially profound, where he
stands on a wire
so far above the street
he might be no more than
a mere bird alight in our
consciousness. But
damn! he will remind us
just so, as we
feel a clench in the
gut, that even with our
feet fastened firm
to the pavement, we
remain afraid
of falling.

Calder

Because the dance
is gone almost
at once—this day's sun—everything—
mutable. What is, now, now and
now; because the body
wants, because the
mind needs
stasis, something
to hang on to. Two birds now,
sparrows, swoop
from one corner
of the roof, up
under the eaves.
It is the
arc the mind wants, its
geometry, how it is
scribed on air.
How many
words are needed then
to pin a shape to something
less fallible than
self? Time
the only problem, its
motion, its insistent *removal*
of everything (even the arc
invented, any bird
being only *here*, then,
here) and the mind wanting
only to make a fist, to
clutch, to hold.

Window with Crow

(Finding the little bird under the snow, the child said, *oh small angel, little frozen mummy, what do you hold in your stilled stone heart?* But it was the crow who replied from an unseen perch, *only time, child, only time.*)

Almost any window
might contain a crow—not
some taxidermist's misplaced
joke with morning coat and spectacles—something
more like those that filled Van Gogh's head
at Arles. Or perhaps only
a still-life with bottles, illuminated
by a simple blessing
of late-afternoon
light.

And a violin, without
music. Unstrung,
it knows only
the dry voice of the crow.

Stiff-bristled, flightless bird,
allegory run amok. Bottles of light
corked for centuries. What
besides memory presses against
the glass? There is no name
for the buzzing between your ears.

Here is the voice,
sounded in sleep. *Spend*
everything you have. Fallen,
you shall plant the seeds again.
It was crow who brought corn
to the people. It was crow who said,
grow this, make it better than it is;
I will return for the harvest.

❖

What you remember from tramping those fields—
the slanting autumn light, the pungent bite
of a shotgun shell, recently fired.

❖

But maybe the light
is on *this* side
of the window; maybe
there *is* no out there.
And we are left with only
an inference: stringless
fiddle, wingless bird.

Grapes

Pulled
from its woody
stem, each
makes a barely
audible pop; corpuscular,
turgid, they bounce
into the colander, deep
bruised blueblack against
white bowl in this
morning light, in this
very ordinary most amazing
day. And if these are not
worthy of your attention; if
this is not, after all, what
you came for, then
tell me, what is it
that you are
expecting, now,
in this
life?

Water Lilies

Start with
white light.
Not differentiated, not
yet passed through any
lens—inconceivably everything
that is, or
could be.

Before the rain—cloudlight
recalling the smell
of earth, glancing from the surface
of a shallow vernal pool. Hands
clasped behind our backs, we peer
into what the mind makes water,
and accept again, as always,
the veracity of illusion.

Consider that he had to *build*
the pond, moving earth, pouring
concrete, cajoling the delicate
watercourse. Only when that work

was done, and the plantings
given time to soften the toolmarks,
only then could he lean into
the fierce canvas, pursuing the light
from layer to layer to layer.

❖

It is the trick of a lens
after all—light coerced into focus, sorted
by wavelength to seemingly yield
information. But remove the lens and,
bottle-blind, confront the brightness
that is everything
and nothing.

❖

Is it water or is it light? this stuff
in which everything hangs suspended?

❖

This particular present then, invented
by lens and retina and neural network,
so eloquently pretending the leatherbrown
oak leaves, the glistening webstrands
windborne everywhere, the honed steel surface

of the reservoir below this glowing hill,
so that it is impossible not to believe
in the ruby meadowhawk dragonfly
which has just landed on my pantleg,
its thorax pulsing with *now*.

❖

Carefully, he opens the box containing the world
and finds inside
nothing.

❖

Nothing
but
light.

❖

A child then, with the parts of a clock
spread out across the table; where is
time?

Here, the pocketful of marbles
I *haven't* lost—the clacking sound
of their collisions—my inference
of meaning. But where is the photon
now? Who is calculating
its path? Light trapped in water
still waiting to be.

❖

How many layers do you think
lie beneath the surface? of the pond? of
the painting? of the light glancing
off pigment? of your own
retinal field? of the neural map that pretends
this image into being? How many layers
do you think it takes to make
a world? How many?

String

Somewhere
it balls up to occupy
a definable space, or else
it does, in fact, have an
end, though no one living
has seen it. In the imagined mountains
where ancient snowpack gives rise to the rivers of the world,
it congregates itself without
need of explanation. Wound around
time's finger, it remembers, then forgets
itself. There is so much
it must hold together.

Coiled in the springs of a thousand
clocks, it may be snared by escapement and
bitten off into finite lengths, where
you find it sometimes,
unexpected, on the forest floor, perhaps,
buried in dark pungent humus, or
up in the canopy of leaves
intertwined with branch-tangle, or maybe even
in the water—a glimpse only—
amid the flashing roil of a snowmelt stream.

❖

Listen. There is nothing
new here. Each breath connected
to the last. So that we
become ourselves again and
again, each word carrying us
where we have not
been, gates of the
temple always just
out of reach. If you find
the string, grab it;
flip a coin; move
in one direction
or
the other.

Valentine

if this is a color, then perhaps something
like lavender or that other—ashes of rose.
culminate   culminates   culminating.   everything
in the mail already.   Rockport.
Tuesday.   sciatica.   three small
ivory buttons wrapped in kleenex
at the very back of the drawer.   forgiveness
lapidary   how the moonsnail grips
the rock.   postmark   promise   moneyclip
what it means finally to say
she was left alone at the last
with her memories.

Balloon

Blare
of a trumpet—single
note strident against the blue
sky. Your life much more
than half gone. If there is
a place to stop on this road
you have forgotten
where. A sky so full
of arabesque. Magritte's coat
hung out to dry, and people
too, waving from the basket now
as if this day would last
forever.

Joe's Barn

Dusk, some lavender
in the sky seen
through this wide high
door. Corner of the house with the blue
shingles—you know the one
I mean—consider the lean
of its chimney, to the opposite
direction from the small tree, which must
arch away from the house
to find growing room;
consider the mode of its
weathering, here in this quiet
yard where it is only
itself. This is the state of mind
of the looking exercise, the
finding the words to see
exercise, but now
it is already darker,
the lavender moving toward
mauve, the blue toward blueblack
night and I haven't yet mentioned
the rough grass, the picnic table
with its benches, the
clothesline, the three
white
chairs.

Vigil

for Stanley Kunitz

Here is something
I never would have told
you: sometimes, waking
in the cold eye of 3 a.m.
I would imagine you,
sitting there in Provincetown or
New York, your face luminous
in a small pool of light afloat on the
deep black silence, your thin fingers
moving carefully over a page,
and stopping now, to smooth out
a wrinkle
in the dark descending
night.

III

The President Embraces Global Warming as the Antidote to Fluctuations in the Marketplace

What was
that? he said, unfolding
his lawn chair at the edge
of the precipice. Oh we've got a fine
circus here, she said, we're just
warming up our old calliope. We got
some weather here will knock
your hat off. We crank up the
juice, you're gonna feel
the firmament
dance.

Refusal: 9/12/2001

This poem will not wear
the flag today. This poem
stunned to silence by history, will not
become part of the pregame peptalk, will not
be purchased by the quick need for blood,
will not be cajoled into extolling war.

This poem will not resort to nostalgia,
seizing opportunity to borrow exalted words
from the distinctly glorified past. This
poem, however bruised and battered,
seemingly knocked irreparably from
its mooring of meaning, will not
engage in the easy self-aggrandizement
of nationalism to assuage its guilt and anger.

While the greasy smoke still stains
the sunrise, while the dust is still
borne aloft like volcanic ash, while
the dead remain uncounted, this poem
will rise gingerly in the landmine
field of words, constituting itself
only slowly out of silence. Against
all odds, this poem will try again
to learn to pray.

The Sound of Glass

I

If even marble angels weep
they must do so in their own stone
voices, and at a frequency so low
we cannot hear. And yet I think
that this might be the hidden music
that lies beneath the motion of our days.
Speed up the movie on a cosmic scale
until our collective voice becomes a high-pitched
warble, and you might hear the low keening
that weds their tears to history.

In a darkening wood, in a lost century,
a child weeps before the terrible ovens. And she
is not alone; all the fearful portals hide their
victim souls. Yet this is not a graveyard,
where the past is laid to rest, marked only by a
polished stone. These terrors do not surrender
at last to the residuary worm, but like the worm itself
fester and multiply in the fecund dark until
even innocent airliners scribe the sky
with deadly perfect arcs, and all the holy cities
bloom with bombs.

II

Excerpts from The Kamikaze Flight Manual[*]

Transcend life and death. When you eliminate
all thoughts about life and death, you will be able
to totally disregard your earthly life.

Your speed is at maximum. The plane tends to lift.
But you can prevent this by pushing the elevator control
forward sufficiently to allow for the increase in speed.

Do your best. Push forward with all your might.
You have lived for 20 years or more. You must exert
your full might for the last time in your life.

Just before the collision it is essential that you do not
shut your eyes. Many have crashed into the targets
with wide-open eyes. They will tell you what fun they had.

You feel that you are suddenly floating in the air.
At that moment, you see your mother's face.
She is not smiling or crying. It is her usual face.

You feel that you smiled at the last moment. You may nod then,
or wonder what happened. You may even hear a final sound
like the breaking of crystal. Then you are no more.

---

[*] Extracted from the translation in *Kamikaze: Japan's Suicide Gods* by Albert Axell and
Hideaki Kase. London: Longman, 2002. Used by permission.

III

You have then as in photographs
the nightmare images: the emaciated
and broken bodies of the damned
laid out on planks for your inspection;
the children whose flesh was roasted
on their bones by flaming plastic
from the sky; the severed body parts
that litter all these named and unnamed fields.

This is the fatal thing that we have learned:
Family. Band. Tribe. Nation. The making of
flags, speeches, armies. Carthage.
Towton. Gettysburg. Hiroshima. Already
the dead mount up like cordwood
behind the house. Who is counting
the corpses now? This after all
is what history demands of us: to fill the only vessel
we think will hold our name.

Yet at the very last we hope to dream our mother's face,
fading into our own faint smile, and hearing only
the small and distant sound of glass.

Rant for a Rusty Kazoo

America, I hear
your singing and I hear your
self-satisfied after-dinner
belch and I hear your secret
midnight fart. And I'm sitting here,
America, taking some ease in
the cool of morning and I know
I'm complicit as hell. America,
we had this all out four decades ago.

America,
we made a bargain—I would stop
shouting obscenities from your
rooftops and you
would stop parading burning children
on the evening news. And you stopped
for a time at least, dropping the terrible
euphemisms from the sky;
pretended at least
to learn something like
humility. And I? Adrift in this graying
climate, gave up the soapbox and the pen,
found booze or coke or money
certain enough distractions, grew up,
invented something like a life. America,
what happened? Did we both
come somehow to believe

that we were entitled to the easy gait
with which we waltzed through
the century's end?

America, why is it always
the narrow-minded, ego-inflated mythic self
that gets to run the show? America, what
is that smell now like gas
leaking in under all the doors.

America,
I'm old now; my gut
complains; my eyes are slow to focus. I want only
to believe in Alex Trebek and the poetry
of a perfect curveball; I want to shop
at WalMart without guilt. America,
why, oh why, must you and I
take up again this slow,
agonizing, and ultimately futile
dance?

Boundary Street

air this morning treed
like a cat.   nothing will come
down.   military industrial
complexity.   my toothbrush
needs batteries.   there is a
grinding noise everywhere.   nothing,
absolutely nothing, is sacred.   especially
these words, written on napkins, stuffed
into the bottom drawer of a
sinking ship.   my wife will not speak
to me; she thinks it's all my
fault.   seven a.m.—already too hot; my shirt
sticks to my back.   even with his flame
at full force, the pilot can't get
altitude; the balloon
drops
into the lake.

The Face That Will Not Come Off

I

Where the light breaks—
mirror, window, the shattered
surface of the world.
Any handle will do
to begin—this day's sun
glances off ice, blinds
drivers heading east, makes
everything a question.
In medias res—there is no
map; the guns are
loaded already. Should I turn on
the radio now? Will there be
instructions? Even with sunglasses
it is impossible to see
into this glare. In the glove compartment
there is a manual for evacuating
the city; it says nothing about
where to begin. Must we
just keep driving then? past
everything? These fields for instance,
now abandoned to weeds, or
these burned-out husks of houses.
Which road are we on? Is there anything
up ahead? beyond all of this
evidence? What is remembered
then, like a story

someone is telling in the next
room, only the rise and fall of the voice
audible. But does it matter?
where we have been? where
we are going? There is only
the road. There is no map.

II

Here beside the highway, soldiers
conducting exercises have left
the remains of their victims.
Flyblown, beyond recognition, they
would have us stop, to offer at least
a prayer. Dare we stop then? The road
is narrow; there is no
shoulder and we are not certain
we remember any prayers.

III

But then I am moving again
without warning, without
preparation, into the cold air called
January fourteenth, into this
day against which I push with my palms,
wincing from old wounds.
Is there a passage? a wormhole?
made of what? Is it
language? Reproducible?
Words only? on a page? Or
spoken perhaps, silently, a sort of
chant whose rhythm forms

a tunnel. What I read just
now, for instance, how they pinched
the girl's cheeks, made her stand
on tiptoe to look
older, and not sickly
as Mengele made
his selection. Perhaps
no tunnel; but
words, all woven into a fabric;
continuous, without selvedge,
perhaps somewhere it
frays, a thread pulled here and
there, small snags which catch
the heel, so that we tumble,
witless, into history.

Jihad

Juxtaposition is
everything. Matter
believes nothing. The task
is to infuse the world
with meaning. The children
are strapped into the car
with the bomb because faith
is required after all, and because
sacrifice is the only answer
that is not already spoken.

Waking to the Same News

How easily the sharp knife
slices through—the ripe
cantaloupe disgorging itself
onto the drainboard. Tuesday—junk mail
piled on the kitchen table. Laundry
accumulates in the corner;
the paper arrives on the doorstep,
offering no promise. Children,
their spirits stolen, stare blankly
from the page. Wash the spilt seed
down the drain. Think
how carefully the young woman
strapped the bomb beneath
her breasts before entering
the marketplace. Think how little difference
between a melon and a skull.

Groundhog Day

Umbra, penumbra. Delicately
teasing apart the tissue separating
night from day. Thermometer stuck
somewhere below twenty.
Like the gearbox of the car,
earth appears to groan in her
turning. No refugees
on the road now; even blood
forgotten beneath the clots
of rotting snow. Direction learned by rote,
we move in a drowse. History
has no lesson, lies somewhere
beyond the hills. We are left
only to our own devices; this and
the thin brittle hope
of a calendar that creaks forward,
graciously oblivious to us all.

We Who Once Lived in This House of Stars

Whoever and whatever you are, we too, once lived in this house of stars, and we
thought of you.

—*Timothy Ferris*

1.

Distance not
withstanding, or is it
time? Our place here
requiring so much
apology. How one makes
a home in the
world. How language
must work hard to keep
that meager foothold; how
the nest is inevitably
fouled by that same
language. None of this
is new—the name for it is
history. How we lived here
the brief time between water and
dust. How the story becomes
in any retelling, a substrate
for belief.

2.

But did not
recognize. Horizon.
Material witness.
What is wanted—
a concrete
explanation—what
you pour over your
cornflakes in the morning.
Instead, a man chained
to the ceiling. Dreamers
and Indians dot the distant
landscape; there is no way
to steer clear of them. We
are running out
of rubber bullets;
the next rounds will burn
real holes.
Pray for us, father,
we know too well
what we do. Our orders
are to aim true. It does not
matter if we tremble; the machine
is large enough
to damp out
small individual
perturbations.

3.

Arrives without memory of the
journey. A mind empty as
pockets. What is
history? What is meaning? What
is a word? Blood,
bone and sinew, surely, but is that
enough? Surely
there are rules, formulas specifying required
content. Surely
a reckoning exists somewhere. What is
motion? What is
forward? It is, of course impossible to know both
velocity and
location. There is no
truth that is not
statistical; no home
that is not
expendable.

Good Friday

But what if he were to fall? Leaning
into the set of possible visions, magnifying
and remagnifying any particular
region, this one, say, in which
we live, the one we call
reality. Suppose, leaning from his stool,
absorbed in the infinitesimal view, he
were to lose his balance for a moment,
tip forward, unable to remember where
he was, and fall headlong into
now? Oh, its alright, you say,
we have been preparing for a long
time; we have already cut
the timbers; we are already striking
the nails.

The juggler

appears on the
horizon. At first only his torso
is visible, surrounded by spinning
knives. He is the new
light of the world. He, surely,
will rewrite the terrible
history. Only later
do we confirm
his crudely
amputated
fingers.

In-Orbit Repairs

if distance. calculated
risk. some of the particulars
are not known. chalice. carbuncle.
in green light everything
glows. all cables must be
mated to the appropriate
adaptor. corollary.
consequence. no room
for error. how can I
steady my hands?
here? in this univers-
al deployment? breathing
room. anathema. cold
comfort, going down.

Versailles

quatrefoil. omnivorous. a world
partially manifest. water,
rust-stained, spent moon leaching into
the haze. circumspect. avaricious.
each voice overshadowed by another
voice. oscillation. propinquity. capital
improvements. swan patrolling
the mouth of the cove like a frigate. this
is the promise made on waking—everything
leaning from center.   gargoyles
pissing in the wind.

Etude at 3 a.m.

stroke of luck. stroke. and
stroke. hard to make port
by morning this way. glass
neither half nor half. my
face reflected from the
other side. so that.
each breath a metaphor embracing
prayer. rain rattling
the windows. change. change
again. curled tight into
the coil of sleep. fulcrum. peabrain.
miniscule voice.
I am.

9/11/2009

That voice—a whisper
on waking—what
is your sorrow? The eyes
of the departed. Long
corridor. Minute flecks
of light—like stars; impossible
to move toward them.
On the town common a man
is raising the flag; the pulleys squeal
as he reverses direction,
then slowly lowers the limp
rag.

Flashlights

Someone said they
made all the difference, started
a movement, lighted the
streets of Copenhagen and
Paris. I'm not so sure; I'm
only here for a short time,
can't seem to catch my
breath. I have dismantled all
the clocks, carefully sorting the parts
into appropriately labeled bins. Here
are the hands you lost in the
war, and a pallet
for you to lie down on. There are
enough springs to restore hope
to your remaining years. I
can no longer stay; the portion
of god's shawl into which my name
is stitched is raveled beyond
recognition. Already
my breath blows the leaves
from the trees. Already the wind
has forgotten my voice.

IV

Spring in the Emerald City

Air almost too
warm this morning and
something else, not quite
palpable, as if some unseen machine
were whirring away to make
this day—simulation almost
too real. As if each leaf were unfolding
specifically to realize the expression
of its own math; as if the very edges
of the world comprised, above all,
an answer. Is this what Adam
saw that first morning, waking
to the wonder of a made world?
Oh, but here we know that the apple
has already been eaten; our libraries
are filled with the accounting of broken
commandments. We are still looking
for the loophole. This morning perhaps only
a reprieve, engineered from carefully compiled
historical data. May six—it looks
like this.
Exactly.

Reading Michele's Book on a Train Late at Night

...Reflected
in the glass, a lesser chaos—my pulse
tracing itself in green moonlight.
— M. Wyrebek, *Be Properly Scared*

The surprise is that I can
bear it, or think I can—this thing
we all must do, just now as close
as the moon of my thumbnail. How much
already is surrendered: keen sight,
for instance, and the fine peppered
taste of vigor. I can feel
the silent popping of tiny stitches
here and there—old coat seams
giving way. So many names for terror
hidden in the flesh.

                    Outside
some portion of the Carolinas
dissolves in swamp and wood and
deepest unguent dark. Somewhere
I imagine an owl. Its hooded yellow
eye fixes time to the broad
curving back of night. This breath,
I think, and the next
are enough
to hold
the world.

Brief Journey Through the Visual Cortex

Splashed
against the retinal
surface. Firmament.
Lens from the
inside (dream of the
Kamikaze pilot, or Icarus in his seaward
plunge). Consciousness bound
to any substrate. What
we will construct. There is no
prescription; there is no
ground of intention, no place
for it to live. Last
gasp. The metaphor named
knowledge; the metaphor
named *God*.

Prime Meridian

It is impossible to say where
the wall ends and the woman begins,
stone and flesh being similar forms
of camouflage. Language still
unspoken, and yet this music
must exist somewhere—more than a voice heard
in dream (how the woman seems
to emerge from the wall sometimes, an arm
or a hip briefly discernable against
the rough surface). Somewhere
it matters profoundly
that there are vowel sounds, round
on the tongue of memory.

When the woman in the wall dreams,
worlds evolve in the susurrations
of her breath. Tectonic plates
glide together into continents, algae
bloom in warm new seas, and matter begins
the spiral dance that animates the world. Neurons
invent themselves and link and link and
link to weave the rich brocade
that yet becomes her dream.

How her mind moves out along the arc
of the ecliptic, still seeking new
connections. How we sense
her presence everywhere—stone ruins
now engulfed in woods, angels
with weathered wings, funerary urns
inscribed to those forgotten—or simply sunlight
on old plaster, texture of dreaming, the evidence
of her longed-for touch.

When the woman inside the wall speaks,
it is as if the room itself were speaking;
echoes over the wide floorboards; light
of another century through the high
arched windows; a name whispered
for the very last time. Whatever
is written will be lost; architecture
reduced to geometric
abstraction; the light of even
the most distant stars
already arriving.

When the woman in the wall sleeps
night enshrouds us with forgetting.
The rivers rise in the dark to whisper
at our doors. The owl is forsaken; we reach
deeper and deeper into our pockets
to find the moon.

Entr'acte

See here young
saxophone, everything's
adrift in this domesticated
maelstrom. Car keys
in the bird's nests; cookware
in the grand piano; the sequined breath
of giants rounding the corner
like freight trains. This prestidigitation
is penultimate; afterwards,
just the curtains
flapping
in hot
vermillion
wind.

Argument in Favor of Existence

On the way to the door then. A hole
in your voice. Easily rattled. Because.
Not only the laws of physics. Non-
being is not. Dream, clearly, the wrong
metaphor. As if someone were to ask, *what's*
for dinner. If you are in the next room
there is no answer. Like clockwork. All
well and good. Without circumstance. No,
without circumference. On the lake, just
now: two fishermen in a red
canoe.

Is it Still Day on the Other Side of the Mirror?

The shoes were called
spectators. What she wore—
a suit? navy? no a light
tan perhaps, to go with
the shoes. It was the train then
—to San Francisco, the first time
you saw that strange light
after the rain...

no

it was not like that at all—
brown and white shoes,
Sunday, the seagreen sky.

Before She Opens Her Eyes

incandescence   entanglement
lightning flashes over the
retinal plane   pinecone   pinwheel
porcupine   a voice without
body   atmospheric incantation
labyrinth   corollary   orchestra
what the next sound will be   and
the next   a structure of inverted
geometry   mortuary   snowflake
candelabrum.

Legal Tender

Omigod, it's
apothecary. And
already morning in this
sarcophagus where the living
is easy. But there's no
writing paper; you have to
remember everything (now
the maggots grow fat
on poetry). Hard choices
there, buster, but what
did you expect
from such a rustic
little theater? Better grab
your homunculus and run
for the nearest exit before
they get your name on their
list. Sign over the door reads "no
rewrites allowed." The coins
in your pocket have already
turned to dust.

Chimera

The trick, he said
while turning a sprightly
pirouette, *is to supplant*
one obsession with
another. Sleight of
mind say; a simple dance. Nothing,
after all, is permanent. Snapping
fingers now as if even
tomorrow were trivial, (look, this
is what I have collected—poof—up
in smoke), dismissed
with another deft spin. *Of course*
you can always
start again, can't you? I ask, but
he has turned away
now, the bright beam
of his being
directed
elsewhere.

The Landscape at Two O'clock

...the look in her eye
when... or the color of the wind
on your cheek—a negotiable
fiction; everything
imagined already—wallpaper
peeling from the wall; a kitchen
in too much sunlight; the child
home from school, believing
everything. There are no dogs
in this story, or cats either, although
there might be a goat, standing
quietly in the next room, eating
the furniture. Coins spread
like lies across the table. Words
line your pockets like spent
kleenex. You still don't know
what to pack for the journey.

There Goes the Neighborhood

I filled my coffee mug and left it on the sink. That
was Tuesday. It was before the rain stopped; before
Albuquerque, before all of the edicts of the recent
past. I have no idea where I put my ticket. My pockets
have rearranged themselves and I don't recognize
the name pinned to my shirt. The man
riding the lawnmower in neat circles appears
to know where he is going. I am wondering if it's true
that I still remember how to ride a bicycle.

Euclidian

Calyx. Corona. Chimera.
Why the pattern is always
in threes. For instance
Tuesday. The man crossing
the highway, a strong diagonal
tying together the disparate parts
of the collage. Vermillion accent
in the curve of his collar.
We have learned to largely disregard
the traffic, background noise
to our daily lives. Corollary.
Exigency. Physical
attraction. Seven dark rectangles
with complicated geometry. Nothing
standing still; no point from which
position can be
triangulated. It is nineteen
minutes past eight.

Closing the Camp

Finally then. Whateveritis.
This moment. Log added
to the woodstove; how long
you might expect. to live.
Tell me again, please,
is it the blue toothbrush that is mine
or the red? More like music
perhaps—a quartet—resolution
occurring *between* the lines. Is it
always so easy to say exactly
what you mean? Context. Sub
text. Counterpoint. How many
blankets we might pile
on the bed against the early
October chill. This collective
enterprise, this drawn breath, this
implacable illusion of meaning.

Some mornings

the mind wakes up
before the body, and
surveying the near
future, rebels, folds itself
neatly, like a clean
handkerchief, hoping to sleep
undisturbed in a dark
pocket.

Old Penny

light dissolves in the flow of each
breath. we dream without color. windowshades.
antimacassars. long hallway with rain
at both ends. everything contained here
in the mortal coil. chameleon. farmwagon.
dark, earnest, tears.

Purple Hologram

Did you
get that? Sound
of wind? Whispered
incantation? Dawn
reflected in my grandfather's
glass eye (why this
was written in the first
place). There are few roads
in this country and
all of the trails are
imaginary. Clearly,
we are here at our own
risk. Shall we begin
then? The future is already
rolled up and put away, the past
still waits. Somewhere,
down a dark hall,
a child is singing,
amazed by his own
voice.

Winged Seed

echinoderm. latchhook. particularity. the voices
inside—the voices outside. everyone
elsewhere. three inches of rain in two days. calumny.
ornithopter. the pretense of meaning.
in this dark hallway. god's eye
in my skull. reluctant necessity of flesh. an old car
foundered in new floodwaters. from
fear. persimmon. polyglot. wrong end
of the marble. explain yourself? a substance
made of ephemeral events. how indeed
to swim through the hole in the sky.

After the Internecine Wars

The ice-cream stand is
closed for the winter but this
does not stop the children's
tantrums. The mother
is using a wide brush to paint
the ceiling with silence. Not yet
January and already
two good storms and two messy
thaws. Anyone who can find work
has likely done so. It will take
several days to assess the damage
from the ruptured coal-sludge dam. Even
where it is not wanted, the truth
tends to muscle its way in the
door. Door is like doom with a different
ending. She wonders if she can return
the unused paint to the store.

Write When You Can

The lady wearing weeds
appears at the gate demanding
yesterday. But the houses
are already on fire. It is impossible
to counter the pull of the moon. If
you were married to her, he thinks, time
would last forever.

This Light, Exalted

See,
the clouds themselves
cast shadows. It is the same
beneath the moon. Already
I have spent my allotment. Oh but
nevermind that; this is not
about me.

You see the difference—there is still
open water, just there
where the street runoff feeds
the lake. This morning,
five ducks.

There is no reward
for any of this. Name
of the landlord erased
from the agreement. Words only,
fickle as weather.

The surprise is that I can mean
exactly what I am saying, here
in this bone closet, my prison.

Snow falling from the trees—
in my mind it makes a sound
like glass.

Prognosis

Coming late,
these words miss
the point, remain imprisoned
in their own expectation. I
have already climbed
the mountain; my pockets
are filled with mist. Later,
if you seek me, look
among the hard stones
of the trail, or the knotted
roots of the pines where they
cling to exposed rock. That
is what my mind
is becoming
now.